300
Incredible Things
for Travelers
on the
Internet

300INCREDIBLE.COM, LLC
600 Village Trace, Building 23
Marietta, Georgia 30067

(800) 909-6505

ISBN 0-9658668-6-6

Introduction

This book is for people who love to travel, and these Web sites will help travelers research, plan and arrange all types of trips. Many of the sites can also be used to experience places you may never have the opportunity to visit in person. Students and others will find this book useful for learning about the world around them. So, log on and travel the World Wide Web!

Ken Leebow
Leebow@300INCREDIBLE.COM
http://www.300INCREDIBLE.COM

About the Author

Ken Leebow has been in the computer business for over 20 years. The Internet has fascinated him since he began exploring its riches a few years ago, and he has helped thousands of individuals and businesses understand and utilize its resources.

When not on the Net, you can find Ken playing tennis, running, reading or spending time with his family. He is living proof that being addicted to the Net doesn't mean giving up on the other pleasures of life.

— Dedication —

To my wife, Denice, who handles our travel plans
and always insures smooth sailing.

Acknowledgments

Putting a book together requires many expressions of appreciation. I do this with great joy, as there are several people who have played vital roles in the process:

- My kids, Alissa and Josh, who helped identify some of the cool sites.

- My wife, Denice, who has been patient with me while I have spent untold hours on the Internet.

- Paul Joffe and Janet Bolton, of *TBI Creative Services*, for their editing and graphics skills and for keeping me focused.

- The multitude of great people who have encouraged and assisted me via e-mail.

- Mark Krasner and Janice Caselli for sharing my vision of the book and helping make it a reality.

Books by Ken Leebow

300 Incredible Things to Do on the Internet

300 Incredible Things for Kids on the Internet

300 Incredible Things for Sports Fans on the Internet

300 Incredible Things for Golfers on the Internet

300 Incredible Things for Beanie Lovers on the Internet

300 Incredible Things for Travelers on the Internet

America Online Web Site Directory
Where to Go for What You Need

TABLE OF CONTENTS

TABLE OF CONTENTS (continued)

CHAPTER I
TRAVEL FIRST CLASS

1
Condé Nast Traveler

http://travel.epicurious.com
Condé Nast provides everything a traveler needs…from bookings to weather.

2
Preview Travel

http://www.previewtravel.com
http://destinations.previewtravel.com
From destinations to reservation guides, you'll find it all here.

3
Trip.com

http://www.thetrip.com
Track flights and view hotel, restaurant and weather information for particular cities.

4
Travelocity
http://www.travelocity.com
Make airline reservations, check airfares, request the lowest price and more.

5
Travel with Microsoft
http://expedia.msn.com
Microsoft's travel site is one of the best on the Net.

6
Business Traveler
http://www.biztravel.com
If you travel for business, check this site out. You can track flights in progress, learn about cities throughout the world, get directions, obtain your frequent flyer miles (not all airlines are available) and a lot of other stuff.

7
Rules of the Air

http://www.1travel.com
For the #1 traveler, here's a site that will provide you information on "rules of the air" and deals on all types of travel.

8
Atevo

http://www.atevo.com
Travel guides, reservations, tips and more are waiting for you.

9
TravelScape

http://www.travelscape.com
At this site, make airline reservations, look up airfares and, best of all, check out the destination guides.

10
Leisure Planet

http://www.leisureplanet.com
Go here and check out all of the cities you can visit. You might even want to book a trip.

11
Travel with Yahoo!

http://travel.yahoo.com
Let Yahoo!'s travel guides assist you with your next trip.

12
Travel Specials

http://www.travelhub.com
TravelHub says, "One site, hundreds of agencies and thousands of specialties."

13
Leisurely Planning

http://www.leisureplan.com
You'll find travel guides, a world event calendar and a place to book your trip.

14
City Guides

http://cityguide.lycos.com
http://www.lycos.com/travel
The Lycos city guide has detailed information about cities around the world.

15
Travel File

http://www.travelfile.com
Type in a city, and see what you get: accommodations, sites to see, restaurants and more.

16
Links A–Z

http://links.expedia.com/am
Click on a city, and you will find information about it here.

17
Your Travel Page

http://www.travelpage.com
Whether you are traveling for leisure or business, this site can provide information that will help you decide where to go and how to get there.

18
World Travel Awards

http://www.worldtravelawards.com
Which are the best? There are over 100 award categories (airline, hotel, resort, etc.). Take a look; you'll find many great travel ideas.

19
Travel Scorecard
http://www.gomez.com/Travel/Scorecard
Gomez, which are the best travel sites of them all?

20
The Travel Shop
http://www.travelshop.de/english.htm
You'll find airlines, airports, hotels, cruises, travelogues and more at this site.

21
Travel in Health
http://www.travelhealth.com
http://www.drwisetravel.com
Get everything you need for your trip online…except the shots.

22
The Internet Travel Agency
http://www.internettravelagency.com
Visit this virtual travel agency.

23
Agent Search
http://www.astanet.com/search
Use the American Society of Travel Agents Web site to find a travel agent.
There's lots of other good travel information here as well.

24
Travel Light
http://www.oratory.com/travel
Doug says, "A compendium of opinions and ideas on the art of travel, with an emphasis on living out of one (carry-on-sized) bag." A lot of good advice here.

25
Don't Leave Home Without It

http://travel.americanexpress.com
American Express knows travel.

26
It's a Zoo Out Here

http://www.travelzoo.com
This site pools together vacation bargains and travel deals from a large variety of sources. Visit the zoo and see if it has a deal for you.

27
Travel Now!

http://www.travelnow.com
TravelNow wants you to search for the best airfares, book hotel reservations and rent a car all with the convenience of your computer.

28
Show Me the Money

http://www.mastercard.com/atm
http://www.visa.com/pd/atm/main.html
Need to locate an ATM? Find it here.

29
Currency Conversion

http://www.x-rates.com
http://www.oanda.com
http://www.traveloco.com/tools/xenon.html
http://www.dna.lth.se/cgi-bin/kurt/rates
If you're traveling to another country, you will want to print out a simple currency conversion cheat sheet. Let these sites help.

30
Better Late Than Never
http://www.lastminutetravel.com
Want to find out what kind of deals are offered if you're a last minute traveler? Here's the site that was designed for you.

31
Yahoo! Takes Off
http://yahoo.flifo.com
Yahoo is now in the travel business. You can book flights and find out arrival and departure times.

32
Total Travel
http://www.totaltravel.net
History, travel guides, news and a lot more await you at this very detailed site.

33
Subway Navigator
http://metro.ratp.fr:10001/bin/cities/english
If you're visiting a city with a subway system, make sure you are familiar with the underground world.

34
Wishing You a Great Trip
http://www.bluemountain.com
http://www.123greetings.com/travel
Got a friend who is going away? Then send them a "wishing you a great trip" e-greeting.

35
Ticked Off
http://www.ticked.com
Clean, credible cutting edge travel advice for "the ticked-off tourist."

36
Female Persuasion

http://www.women-traveling.com
http://www.women.com/travel
Women Traveling Together states, "Our goal is to bring women together who want to travel and make new friends, in a comfortable, small group environment while eliminating the penalties of solo travel."

37
The Greatest Places

http://www.greatestplaces.org
Here are seven places you might never have a chance to visit: The Amazon, Greenland, Tibet, Iguazu, Madagascar, Okavango and Namib. Check them out online.

"Our best get-away rate is $19.95 per person. For that price, we'll take your picture and e-mail it to seven different countries of your choice."

38
Weather.com
http://www.weather.com/travelwise
One of the most important things when traveling is the weather. Let the Weather Channel keep you informed about this favorite topic of conversation.

39
Historical Weather
http://www.worldclimate.com
http://www.weatherpost.com/historical/historical.htm
This database offers a huge amount of weather details for over 2,000 cities.

CHAPTER II
IN THE AIR, ON LAND AND SEA

40
Be Wise

http://www.airwise.com
Let this site be your airport and air travel guide.

41
Airlines on the Web

http://www.flyaow.com
http://airtravel.about.com
If it isn't located here, then it doesn't fly. Happy travels.

42
Everything Airplane

http://www.airliners.net
If you travel by air, you will probably enjoy this site, which has a wealth of information about all types of airplanes.

43
Quick Airport Info

http://www.quickaid.com
http://www.airlines.com/directory.cfm
http://www.uni-karlsruhe.de/~un9v/atm/ase.html
For most of the major airports, you will find: transportation, airport maps, hotel, airline and yellow pages information.

44
1-800 Airlines

http://www.princeton.edu/Main/air800.html
http://www.travel-watch.com/airphones.htm
Get a quick listing of many airlines' 800 numbers and Web sites.

45
The Best and Lowest Fares

http://www.bestfares.com
http://www.lowestfare.com
http://www.lowairfare.com
http://www.air-fare.com
http://www.cheaptickets.com

We all know it can be expensive to fly. Get the best possible fare by using these sites.

46
Pick Your Price

http://www.priceline.com

Priceline is changing the airline industry. You simply tell them what you are willing to pay.

47
Be a Courier

http://www.aircourier.org

If you want to save a lot of money and are flexible with your time, you might want to be a member of the Air Courier Association.

48
Web Frequent Fliers

http://www.webflyer.com

http://www.frequentflier.com

Okay, you're on the plane more than you are online. Well, these sites are designed for you.

49
Sell Them Miles

http://www.smartflyer.com

Do you travel too much? Do you have more miles accumulated than you can use? Then stop by Smartflyer and sell some of them.

50
Healthy Flying

http://www.flyana.com
Diana Fairechild is your complete source for safe and healthy travel information. She will guide you through air travel mazes and pitfalls.

51
Make a Reservation

http://www.reservationdesk.com
You can book a flight at this site, but the coolest feature is a 24-hour airfare ticker that you can place on your computer desktop.

52
I'm Mad As...

http://www.passengerrights.com
...and I'm not going to take it anymore. Complain and learn your rights, all in one place.

53
Aviation Internet Resources

http://www.air-online.com

Airlines, airports, aircraft and a lot more. Make sure you visit this site for great information.

54
Everything Aviation

http://www.landings.com

While this site is designed for the aviation enthusiast, novices will also find interesting and useful material.

55
AAA

http://www.aaa.com

The Automobile Association of America has been assisting millions of folks for years. Check them out online.

56
Auto Rentals

http://www.bnm.com
Here's your guide to over 90 major auto rental companies at over 100 airports. Drive safely!

57
Rent a Car

http://www.hertz.com
http://www.avis.com
http://www.goalamo.com
http://www.nationalcar.com
http://www.budgetrentacar.com
These are some of the major car rental companies. Drive safely, and fill 'er up before you bring it back.

58
Railroad Travel
http://www.amtrak.com
http://www.trainweb.com/travel
Everything you ever needed to know about traveling by train.

59
Cruise Lines
http://www.cruising.org/links.html
You'll find them all listed here.

60
Cruise Merchant
http://www.cruisemerchants.com
Use the merchant's Cruise Wizard to identify the cruise that's best for you.

61
CruiseFinder
http://www.fieldingtravel.com/cf/index.htm
Compare and review ships and all their offerings.

62
The Sea Letter
http://www.sealetter.com
Read a newsletter about cruising the high seas. Happy sailing.

63
Get Cruisin'
http://www.getcruising.com
If you love the open seas, cruise on over to this site.

64
Fun, Fun, Fun
http://www.cruisefun.com
This site will make your cruise planning easier, so you can relax and enjoy.

65
Everyone Has One

http://www.cruiseopinion.com
Looking into a cruise? This site will give you a good analysis of all the ships.

66
Cruise News

http://www.porthole.com
http://www.shipboardcruiser.com
These cruise news sources will keep you current and informed about
your options.

67
Small Ships

http://www.smallshipcruises.com
Not interested in the mega-ships? This site will let you know about many fine
cruises that are more intimate.

CHAPTER III
O, BEAUTIFUL, FOR SPACIOUS SKIES

68
State Connection

http://www.stateconnect.com
http://www.onlinecityguide.com
Where are you traveling in the United States? Search for the city and state, and you will find great information.

69
State Guide

http://www.gomez.com/Travel/Tools
Pick a state, any state, and you will be guided to an informative site.

70
City Link

http://www.usacitylink.com
The USA CityLink Project is a city's interface to the world. It is a comprehensive listing of U.S. States and cities offering information on travel, tourism and relocation.

71
Excited about Travel

http://www.city.net
Excite, the search engine, has a travel site that has tons of great information.

"The beds are lumpy, the shower is drippy,
the television is broken, and my husband is boring!"

72
Going Local

http://local.yahoo.com
http://www.sidewalk.com
http://www.digitalcity.com
http://www.citysearch.com
These sites have a lot of information about cities. If you are traveling, require information about a town or just have a need to know, dive right in.

73
Travelbase

http://www.travelbase.com
Get summary information about traveling in any state.

74
City Guides

http://www.infospace.com
Take a virtual tour with InfoSpace's city guides.

75
Can't Find That Station

http://www.radioguide.com/cities.html

Every time you visit a new city, you probably have to fumble around to find the radio stations that you like. Well, here are complete listings in the top 100 markets in the U.S.

76
Road Construction

http://www.randmcnally.com/tools/construc.htm

Before you head off on that next road trip, check this site out to see if there is any construction going on along the way. There are also many other interesting sites to see while touring this one.

77
I-95

http://www.usastar.com

It's a long road. For anyone traveling from Maine to Miami (or anywhere in-between), let this site be your guide.

78
Slow Down!

http://www.speedtrap.com
Nobody likes getting a speeding ticket. Before you go on the road, check this site out to learn where the speed traps are.

79
Roadside America

http://www.roadsideamerica.com
Your online guide to offbeat tourist attractions.

80
The Big Apple

http://www.nycvisit.com
The official tourism Web site of the New York Convention & Visitors Bureau.

81
New York Streetfinder
http://www.web100.com/~sib/streetfinder.html
This site will allow you to find the nearest cross street for an address on an avenue in Manhattan.

82
New York Mass Transit
http://www.mta.nyc.ny.us/nyct
If you want to get on the subway, train or bus, make sure you stop here.

83
New York's Underground
http://www.nationalgeographic.com/features/97/nyunderground
Want to know what's happening in the "underbelly" of New York? National Geographic gives you a tour of New York's underground, an area that no tour guide will show you.

84
New York Theater

http://www.botz.com/nytheatre

Here's your guide and source for show listings, reviews and more.

85
Playbill

http://www.playbill.com

Theater news, listings and information for Broadway, off Broadway, Summer Stock, London and the rest of the world.

86
New York, New York

http://www.ci.nyc.ny.us
http://www.newyork.digitalcity.com
http://www.citysearchnyc.com
http://www.urbanaccess.com
http://www.shaw-review.com

These sites would make Frank Sinatra very proud.

87
Chicago's Restaurants

http://www.searchchicago.com
Your quick and easy entrée to the best Chicago area reataurants.

88
Washington, D.C.

http://www.washington.org
The official tourism site for Washington, D.C.

89
Las Vegas

http://www.a2zlasvegas.com
http://www.pcap.com/lasvegas.htm
http://www.whats-on.com
What's happening in Vegas? Gambling, shows, dining and more gambling.

90
L.A. Confidential

http://www.la.com
http://www.calendarlive.com
Before you visit the City of Angels, check out these guides for information about entertainment, dining, hotels and more.

91
I Left My Heart in…

http://www.hotelres.com
…San Francisco, of course.

92
The Sunshine State

http://www.flausa.com
http://www.funandsun.com
http://www.floridainfo.com
http://www.see-florida.com
Enjoy the sun and fun in Florida.

93
Orlando

http://www.go2orlando.com
If you're headed for Orlando, you definitely need to bookmark this site. Get the weather, a guide to attractions and much more.

94
Where are You Going Next?

http://www.disneyworld.com
http://www.hotelorlando.com
I'm packing my bags and going to DisneyWorld!

95
Virtually Disney

http://www.intercot.com
Take a virtual tour of Disney World.

96
New England Pride

http://www.newengland.com

"For more than 60 years, Yankee Magazine has been the authority on travel and life in New England. We know the region better than anyone else, and we'd like to help you discover the best New England has to offer."

97
The Smoky Mountains

http://www.thesmokies.com

One of the most beautiful areas in the United States. Go for a visit today.

98
The Biltmore

http://www.biltmore.com

Originally constructed for the Vanderbilts, this magnificent estate is open for visitors in Asheville, NC.

99
Hawaii, Here I Come

http://www.gohawaii.com
http://www.thisweek.com
http://www.maui.net/~tkern/beaches.html
Learn about the beautiful Hawaiian Islands.

100
Alaska

http://www.360alaska.com
Take a tour of Alaska here, and be prepared for a "visual immersion."

101
Sleepless In Seattle

http://www.seattle.net
Lots of great stuff to do in the Emerald City.

102
I Love New Orleans

http://www.frenchquarter.com
http://www.loveneworleans.com
And I'm sure you will, too. If you can't make it to New Orleans, then at least peek at BourboCam, a live shot of Bourbon Street.

103
Escape to Puerto Rico

http://escape.topuertorico.com
Enjoy this great island that may someday become the 51st state of the U.S.

104
Spoleto

http://www.spoletousa.org
Charleston, South Carolina is one of the jewels of the South. If you haven't been there, this annual Spring festival is a good reason to make the excursion.

105
Park Search

http://www.llbean.com/parksearch
http://parks.yahoo.com
http://www.nps.gov
http://www.blm.gov/education
http://parkscanada.pch.gc.ca
Thank you LL Bean, Yahoo!, the U.S. and Canadian governments. These sites have over 1000 parks in their databases.

106
It's Grand!

http://www.thecanyon.com
One of the wonders of the world: The Grand Canyon. Go there right now and send an e-postcard to one of your friends.

107
State Parks
http://www.mindspring.com/~wxrnot/parks.html
Doug has done all the work for you by listing state parks to visit.

108
Rough Guides
http://travel.roughguides.com
You'll find straightforward information on more than 4,000 locations.

109
CNN City Guides
http://www.cnn.com/TRAVEL/CITY.GUIDES
Get a map of just about any city in the world. You can also obtain specific details about many cities.

"If YOU want to fly coast to coast for 75 cents,
that's fine. But I'd feel safer paying full price!"

110
Toronto

http://www.starcitysearch.com
Everything you need to know about Toronto.

111
Montreal

http://www.pagemontreal.qc.ca/meg
http://www.pagemontreal.qc.ca/eindex.html
Experience Montreal.

112
British Columbia

http://www.bctravel.com
The British Columbia Internet Travel Guide covers all the areas you would want
to visit in this beautiful part of the world.

113
Mexico, Here I Come

http://www.wotw.com/mexico
http://www.mexico-travel.com
If you're going to Mexico, make sure you stop here first.

114
Party City

http://www.cancun.com
When in Cancun, do as the tourists do…party on!

115
Caribbean Supersites

http://www.caribguide.com
http://www.where2stay.com
http://www.bermuda-online.com
http://www.caribtravelnews.com
http://www.islandconnoisseur.com
These sites are so good, you'll think you're already in the Caribbean.

CHAPTER IV
IT'S NOT SUCH A SMALL WORLD

116
What's Your Destination?
http://www.infoplease.com/spot/traveldest.html
Where do people go? Here are the top 40 travel destinations around the world.

117
Cameras Around the World
http://www.earthcam.com
Using cameras around the world, you can watch the weather, traffic, resort activities and much more.

118
World Connect

http://www.atlapedia.com
Before you visit a country, you might want to know more about it. This site provides you with all the basics.

119
Traveling to a Foreign Country?

http://www.travlang.com
This site has a lot of valuable information about foreign travel. It also has a translation section that is quite interesting.

120
Voilá!

http://babelfish.altavista.com
Be prepared for your foreign travels. Go to this site, type a word, phrase, or sentence, and it will be translated for you. For example: "My name is Ken Leebow" is "Il mio nome è Ken Leebow" in Italian.

121
Learn That Language!
http://www.accentlanguage.com
Every time you visit a foreign land, you probably wish you knew that native tongue. Now is your chance.

122
What Time is It?
http://www.timeanddate.com
http://tycho.usno.navy.mil/what.html
If you're going out of town, you might need to know the local time.

123
Sunrise, Sunset
http://riemann.usno.navy.mil/aa/data/docs/RS_OneDay.html
Go to this site to learn the times of dawn and dusk for the city of your choice.

124
Plug it In

http://www.kropla.com
Here's a comprehensive listing of worldwide electric current and telephone specifications.

125
Passport, Please

http://www.passportnow.com
http://travel.state.gov/passport_services.html
If you're going abroad and forgot that important document, you might want to check out Passport Now (to get a passport quickly) or the State Department.

126
Customs

http://www.customs.treas.gov
Take the fear out of foreign travel. Consult the Traveler Information section before you take off.

127
U.S. Bureau of Consular Affairs

http://travel.state.gov
http://travel.state.gov/travel_warnings.html
It's a bit stuffy here, but you might need some information from this site. If you are traveling out of the U.S., make sure you find out about any travel warnings, and have a safe trip.

128
The Embassy Page

http://www.embpage.org
Here's a searchable diplomacy database with over 50,000 addresses, phone numbers and e-mail addresses of diplomatic posts worldwide.

129
U.S.A. and Worldwide Tourism Office

http://www.towd.com
http://www.information-usa.com
Before visiting any country or state, you may want to visit its official tourism site.

130
Take Me to Your Leader

http://www.trytel.com/~aberdeen
http://www.geocities.com/Athens/1058/rulers.html
If you're traveling to a foreign country and are curious about its government and leaders, check out these sites.

131
Country Profiles
http://www.washingtonpost.com/wp-srv/inatl/front.htm
http://www.tradeport.org/ts/countries
http://www.wtgonline.com
These sites will keep you posted on all countries.

132
Tax Dollars at Work
http://lcweb2.loc.gov/frd/cs/cshome.html
http://www.odci.gov/cia/publications/factbook
If you're a U.S. citizen, some of your tax dollars pay for this extensive list of countries, including a tremendous amount of detail.

133
Travel.org
http://travel.org/index2.html
This site allows you to find information about many cities throughout the world.

134
Down Under

http://www.citysearch.com.au
http://tourism.gov.au
Visit our friends in Australia. You'll even find an Olympic countdown clock.

135
Visit Europe

http://www.visiteurope.com
http://www.eurodata.com
The European Travel Commission's official Web site has detailed information about 29 European nations. And while you're planning your European vacation, visit Eurodata's online magazine.

136
Hotels in Europe

http://www.eurotels.com
Need a place to stay in Europe? This site will be happy to accommodate you.

137
Europe Through the Back Door

http://www.ricksteves.com
Rick says, "We want to help you make the most of every mile, minute and dollar on your next European adventure."

138
Budget Travel in Europe

http://www.eurotrip.com
If you want reports, advice, information and discussions about budget travel in Europe, here is your site. By the way, it's free.

139
European Auto Travel

http://www.michelin-travel.com
Let the Michelin man help you map out your travel plans for touring Europe.

140
Europe by Air or Train

http://www.eurail.com
http://www.eurairpass.com
Get your Eurail or Eurair pass at these two sites.

141
Pack it In

http://www.backpackeurope.com
Frommer's says, "Definitely the first site you should visit if you plan to 'pack it' across Europe."

142
London Walks

http://london.walks.com
Take a stroll around London.

143
This Is London

http://www.thisislondon.com
http://www.londontown.com
http://www.a-london-guide.co.uk
Get a feel for the local flavor before planning your trip to this incredible city.

144
The British Isles

http://www.britannia.com
Before you go to the British Isles, make sure you visit this gateway to the destinations, attractions and travel methods.

145
Visit Britain

http://www.visitbritain.com
This is the official site of the British Tourist Authority. Tea, anyone?

"For any services provided by our staff, please remember to tip sixty-five percent. It's one of our country's charming exotic customs!"

146
Yahoo! Knows the United Kingdom

http://www.yahoo.co.uk/Recreation/Travel
Yahoo! has a site dedicated to travel in the UK.

147
Dr. Dave's U.K. Pages

http://uk-pages.net
Dr. Dave is retired and lives in Houston. However, you will find he is very knowledgeable and provides excellent information about the U.K.

148
United Kingdom

http://www.ukguide.org
http://www.uktravel.com
http://www.a2btravel.com
http://www.travelengland.org.uk
From A to Z, these sites have tons of information for you.

149
Castles on the Web

http://www.castles-of-britain.com
http://www.castlesontheweb.com
Part of the travel experience is visiting some of the castles of the world.
Check them out on the Net, so you can make plans to see your favorites.

150
France.com

http://www.france.com
http://www.francetourism.com
Ben Franklin said, "Every man has two nations, and one of them is France."

151
Paris

http://www.paris-touristoffice.com
From culture to dining, you'll find it at the tourist office.

152
Pass the Water, Please

http://www.eviantourism.com

Okay, you love Evian water, so, why not visit the city? The pictures at this site look very nice.

153
Spain

http://www.okspain.org
http://www.tourspain.es
http://www.spaintour.com

All your travel needs for Spain are covered at these sites.

154
Italy Online

http://www.initaly.com
http://www.traveleurope.it

When I visit these sites, I just feel like singing and eating.

155
An American in Italy

http://www.hostetler.net
Let Daniel Hostetler, an American living it Italy, tell you all about this magnificant country. Thanks, Dan!

156
Ireland

http://www.ireland.travel.ie
http://www.askireland.com
http://www.irelandseye.com
A land of great castles and tradition.

157
Scandinavian Countries

http://www.goscandinavia.com
This site will take you to the official site of Denmark, Finland, Iceland, Norway and Sweden.

158
Everything Romanian

http://www.rotravel.com
http://travel.necomm.ro
Did you ever want to go to Romania? If yes, go to this site.

159
Asian Travel Guide

http://www.datacomm.ch/pmgeiser/index.html
If you're going on a trip to Cambodia, China, Laos, Myanmar, Tibet, or Vietnam, you'll want to visit here first.

160
Continental Knowledge

http://www.geographia.com
If you plan to visit Africa, Asia, The Caribbean, Europe or Latin America, make your first stop here. You'll get brief but sophisticated information about your destination.

161
Hong Kong

http://www.hkta.org
Going to Hong Kong? This site provides information about planning a trip—the culture, hotels, dining and a lot more.

162
India.com

http://www.iloveindia.com
http://www.tourisminindia.com
You may never actually go there, but now you can make a virtual visit. Also, stop by the Ministry of Tourism's official Web site of India.

163
Virtual Communities

http://www.virtualireland.com
http://www.virtualholyland.com
http://www.virtualjerusalem.com

Virtual Communities, Inc. has three community sites that revolve around Ireland, Israel and Jerusalem, respectively.

164
Tour Egypt

http://touregypt.net

Here's the official tourism site for Egypt. Enjoy the Pyramids and Sphinx.

165
Everything Africa

http://www.africa.com

Africa offers much more than safaris.

166
Safari

http://www.onsafari.com

This site offers information on 50 safari tours. You'll find photos and descriptions of over 100 Safari Lodges and Camps and 50 Game Parks in the countries of Kenya, Tanzania, Zimbabwe, South Africa, Botswana, Zambia and Namibia.

CHAPTER V
TRIP PREP

167
Frommers and Fodors

http://www.frommers.com
http://www.fodors.com
These two publications are widely recognized as the finest travel guides. Sign up for the Frommers free newsletter, and use Fodor's "Miniguides."

168
Brochure

http://www.wwb.com
Here's a listing of more than 15,000 travel maps, guides and brochures.

169
The Travel Search Engine!

http://www.kasbah.com

With over 100,000 hand picked travel sites from 230 countries, you might never leave your computer!

170
Earth to Planet Rider

http://www.planetrider.com

Ride on over to this travel directory of planet earth. It indexes the best sites on the Net. Make sure you visit the "10-minute vacation."

171
Travel Planner

http://www.newsdirectory.com/travel

http://www.newsdirectory.com/news/magazine/travel

This directory has a lot of resources for you. No fancy graphics, just good information.

172
It's a Lonely Planet
http://www.lonelyplanet.com
You'll find destination guides, links by country and other fun stuff.

173
Leisurely Guides
http://www.leisureplanet.com/TravelGuides
Here are some great guides for locations all over the world.

174
Just the Facts
http://www.travelfacts.com
What's hot, auctions, guides, cruises, links and more.

175
Travel Toolkit
http://www.msnbc.com/Modules/Travel/toolkit.asp
MSNBC and Expedia.com's "Travel Toolkit" contains tons of information for you to plan your business or leisure travel.

176
Trip Spot
http://www.tripspot.com
Tripspot is a well-organized site that lists most of the essential travel sites on the Net.

177
Net Travel Guide
http://www.netguide.com/Travel
http://www.zdnet.com/yil/content/depts/useful/usetravel.html
Visit NetGuide and ZDNet for many great sites.

178
Travel Sources

http://www.travelsource.com
http://www.wwtravelsource.com
These two sites will help guide you to many useful travel resources on the Net.

179
Fielding's Travel Guides

http://www.fieldingtravel.com
From dangerous travel to cruises, Fielding's will guide you all the way.

180
Click the Map

http://www.ego.net
http://www.travelpage.com/dest.htm
Click on the map, and find some very good details about your destination.

"So far we've both gained ten pounds on this cruise!
If all the other passengers each gain ten pounds,
how will they keep the ship from sinking?"

181
Find It Here

http://www.travel-finder.com
TravelFinder lets you locate travel information by category, state or province, country or continent.

182
Look Smart

http://www.looksmart.com
Everyone likes to be smart. Go to this site and select the "Your Town" option to instantly go to other sites relating to that town.

183
Mining for Travel Sites

http://marketplace.about.com/travel
About.com will provide you with interesting information about all types of travel.

184
Travel Search

http://www.isleuth.com/trav.html
http://ask.com
Search many of the finer travel sites on the Net.

185
Travel with the Search Engines

http://www.snap.com
http://infoseek.go.com/travel
http://www.lycos.com/travel
http://www.yahoo.com/Recreation/Travel
These search engines and directories provide you with almost limitless possibilities.

186
Travel Tips

http://www.CyberTip4theDay.com
Sign up to get a free travel tip e-mailed to you every day.

187
Travel Secrets

http://www.travelsecrets.com
Learn from the pros. Go to this site, print out the secrets and highlight the ones that interest you. You may save a lot of time and money.

188
1000+ Tips for Trips

http://www.tips4trips.com
From pre-planning to traveling with kids, this site has lots of practical trip tips.

189
Ask Mark

http://www.pathfinder.com/travel/TL/ask/askme.html
Mark Orwoll is a seasoned traveler and managing editor of Travel and Leisure. He will help you with your travel questions.

190
Ask an Expert
http://www.allexperts.com/travel/index.shtml
Isn't it great to ask someone in the know about a travel destination? Here are your travel experts, so go ahead and ask a question.

191
Random Acts of Kindness
http://www.suresite.com/oh/a/armchair
This travel aficionado would like to assist you with your travel plans. Just e-mail her your destination with a few details, and she will provide you with suggestions.

192
Deja Experts
http://www.deja.com/categories/trav.shtml
Go to Deja, and ask fellow netizens anything you want about travel.

193
Travel Tip$
http://www.talks.com/travelarchive.html
Receive travel tips from Auntie Spender. She will even answer your questions.

194
The Shoestring Traveler
http://www.stratpub.com
The e-zine for inexpensive travel. Whether you are traveling on the cheap or not, you will find tons of resources here.

195
Be Smart
http://www.smarterliving.com
This online community site has a newsletter, provides information about discount airfares and offers other travel information.

196
My Travelogue
http://www.travel-library.com
Personal travelogues and worldwide travel and tourism information.

197
All Corners of the World
http://www.travelcorner.com
From the Top 10 cruises to virtual trips around the world, TravelCorner has lots of interesting sites to see.

198
Web Travel Review
http://photo.net/webtravel
The philosophy of this site: "To travel is to live. To live is to travel." Let this photo journalist show you some great shots and spots.

199
Camera, Please
http://www.photosecrets.com/links.html
Photography and travel definitely go together. Let PhotoSecrets link you to great photo information.

200
Road Chip
http://www.roadnews.com
http://pobox.com/~technotravel
If your travel companion is a computer, you might want to check out these sites.

201
The Connected Traveler
http://www.laptoptravel.com
Do you travel out of the country with your laptop computer? If you do, be sure to visit this site first.

202
Family Travel

http://www.familytravelforum.com
Traveling with the kids? Use this site to assist with your plans.

203
Bring the Whole Family

http://www.traveldog.com
http://www.petswelcome.com
http://www.petlifeweb.com/PetInfo/petravel.htm
http://www.ddc.com/waggers/dogs_at_wheel.html
Want to bring your pets along on vacation? Check out this site before checking in.

204
Maps of the World

http://www.nationalgeographic.com/resources/ngo/maps
See a map of just about anywhere in the world.

205
Map it Out

http://www.freetrip.com
http://www.mapsonus.com
http://www.expediamaps.com
http://www.delorme.com/cybermaps/route.asp
Excellent maps and driving directions can be acquired from these sites.

206
MapBlaster

http://www.mapblast.com
This unique site allows you to create a map based on a street address that you provide. One unique feature is that you can then e-mail it to someone.

207
Zippy Directions

http://www.zip2.com
Get the most detailed driving directions on the Net. Also, find out a lot about any city in the U.S.

208
CDC Travel Information
http://www.cdc.gov/travel/index.htm
The Centers for Disease Control wants you to travel safely.

209
Travel Health Online
http://www.tripprep.com
Everything you ever needed to know about healthy traveling.

210
Business Travel Etiquette Club
http://www.traveletiquette.com
http://www.webofculture.com/edu/gestures.html
When you're on foreign soil, business etiquette is important. Stop here before your trip.

211
Road Trip

http://www.asirt.org
The Association for Safe International Road Travel is a not-for profit international humanitarian organization that promotes road travel safety through education and advocacy.

212
Safety Rules

http://www.airsafe.com
http://www.safewithin.com/travelsafe
It never hurts to follow a few simple guidelines when traveling.

213
Rules of the Air

http://www.rulesoftheair.com
Been bumped from a flight? Ever wonder what your options are when your flight is delayed? Need to know just how much luggage you really can check? This site knows the rules.

214
Take a Load Off

http://welcome.to/travelite
Learn how to travel with a little less baggage.

215
Travel Wear

http://www.travelsmith.com
You need to make sure that you have the proper clothes for a trip.
TravelSmith helps you travel lighter and smarter.

216
Buy it Here

http://www.randmcnallystore.com
Before you travel, you must have all the proper paraphernalia. Rand McNally
will be happy to outfit you.

CHAPTER VI
SLEEP, EAT & DRINK

217
All the Hotels on the Web

http://www.all-hotels.com
http://www.hotelsonline.net
http://www.hotelstravel.com
Use these sites to guide you to a hotel of your choice.

218
Hotel Guide

http://www.hotelguide.com
http://www.hotelguide.ch
Your guide to hotels on the Net.

"We can afford a wonderful vacation in Europe,
if we're not too tired from rowing our
canoe across the Atlantic."

219
Hotel Discount

http://www.180096hotel.com
http://www.room-service.net
http://www.hoteldiscount.com
We all want a good deal. Get a discount at these hotels.

220
Can I Stay A While?

http://www.homexchange.com
Staying for a while and don't care for hotels? Go to the International Home Exchange site, and you might find accommodations to your liking.

221
Leading Hotels of the World

http://www.lhw.com
http://pathfinder.com/travel/TL/WldsBest/hotels98.html
If you feel you deserve to stay at the best hotels, then make sure you click on these sites.

222
Hotels and More

http://www.hotelstravel.com
Hotels, airlines, airports and much more can be found here.

223
Hotel Search

http://www.worldhotel.com
Go to this site, type in a location and you will find many of the local hotels listed.

224
Bed and Breakfast

http://www.ibbp.com
http://www.bbchannel.com
http://www.innsandouts.com
http://www.traveldata.com
Learn the ins and outs at these bed and breakfast sites.

225
Hostels

http://www.hiayh.org
http://www.hostels.com
http://www.hostelweb.com
Your complete guide to hosteling and budget travel.

226
Epicurious Food

http://www.epicurious.com
If it has to do with food and drink, you'll find it here.

227
Menus and Food Reviews

http://www.onlinemenus.com
http://www.zagat.com
If you are hungry, look at an online menu. Of course, check Zagat's restaurant reviews first.

228
Let's Eat

http://www.restaurantrow.com
Over 100,000 restaurants in 47 countries. I hope you're hungry.

229
Time Out

http://www.timeout.com
Learn about some of the world's greatest cities—the bars, clubs, hotels, restaurants, shops, galleries, museums and music venues.

230
Food and Travel

http://www.dinesite.com
http://www.dinersgrapevine.com
These sites should help provide a positive dining experience.

231
Cuisine

http://www.cuisinenet.com
You'll find thousands of restaurants located in major U.S. cities.

232
The Road to Food

http://www.eathere.com
Here's a dining guide to over 550 popular roadside diners and restaurants in the United States and Canada.

233
Dinner, a Movie and Popcorn

http://www.dinnerandamovie.com
Just pop in a zip code, and you'll be off to dinner and a movie.

234
On the Road with McDonald's

http://www.vicinity.com/mcdonalds

This site will map out your McDonald's hamburger stops for you.

CHAPTER VII
ATTRACTIONS, RESORTS AND ADVENTURES

235
Travelin' Tunes

http://www.festivalfinder.com
If you love music and travel, check out this site that lists music festivals happening all over.

236
Festival Time

http://www.festivals.com
http://www.holidayfestival.com
These sites will tell you about all types of festivals throughout the world.

237
Culture Vulture
http://www.culturefinder.com
With over 300,000 cultural events listed at this site, you are bound to find something to your liking while on vacation.

238
Museums Galore
http://www.museumca.org/usa
http://wwar.com/museums.html
http://www.elsas.demon.nl/index_e.htm
http://www.dreamscape.com/frankvad/museums.html
Use these sites to guide you to more than 10,000 museums all over the world.

239
Traveling Sports Fan
http://www.cs.rochester.edu/u/ferguson/schedules/cities.html
Do you love sports? Do you travel? Well, here is your site to combine both.

240
SpaFinder

http://www.spafinders.com
Go ahead, pamper yourself with a spa vacation. You'll be able to search here for the one of your choice.

241
Resorts Online

http://www.resortsonline.com
From playing a round of golf to going on a safari, you'll find lots of information here.

242
Rent Me!

http://www.cyberrentals.com
You'll find listings of homes, condos, chalets and other real estate available for rent directly from homeowners and selected rental agencies.

243
Home Sweet Home
http://www.ivacation.com
Find rental properties, homes and timeshares throughout the world.

244
Vineyards
http://www.insiders.com/winecountry
Get the inside scoop on traveling to the wine country.

245
ClubMed
http://www.clubmed.com
Sit back, relax and have tons of fun at one of ClubMed's resorts.

246
Sand, Sun and Fun
http://www.beachcomber.com/Beaches/beaches.html
http://www.petrix.com/beaches/index.html
http://www.oneweb.com/infoctrs/beaches.html
Visit the beaches of the world. And if you can't get there today, check out the WorldCam.

247
Hit the Beach
http://www.hitthebeach.com
Sounds good to me.

248
Best Beaches
http://www.topbeaches.com/list.htm
Goin' to the beach? Here is a list of the best ones in the U.S.

249
Water, Water, Everywhere
http://www.aqueous.com
Here's a search engine dedicated to water related sites. Whether you surf or just loaf, you're sure to find a great spot.

250
Goofing Off with Mickey
http://disney.go.com/Disneyland
http://disney.go.com/DisneyWorld
Pack up the bags, and bring the whole family.

251
Hold on Tight…
http://www.sixflags.com
… when visiting Six Flags.

252
For Adventure...
http://www.4adventure.com
http://www.seaworld.com
...visit Anheuser Busch's adventure Web site.

253
Amusement Parks
http://members.aol.com/parklinks/links.htm
Here's your one-stop source for links to amusement parks around the world.

254
Travel and Learn
http://www.learningvacations.com
Vacations with an educational twist.

"Our credit card was stolen, but I've decided not to report it. The thief is spending less than we did!"

255
Camp Grownup
http://www.grownupcamps.com
Camps are for big people, too! Check out a camp that might be of interest to you.

256
Travel On Dude
http://www.travelon.com
Take a trip to Travelon, and find a vacation that suits your needs.

257
Hey, Dude!
http://www.duderanch.org
Want to feel like a cowboy? Check out the Dude Ranch Association.

258
Goin' Under

http://www.divetravel.com
It's so beautiful. No pressure, come here for a pretty site.

259
Horse Sense

http://www.equestrianvacations.com
If you love horses, then you should check into a vacation on the trails.

260
Goin' to Graceland

http://www.elvis-presley.com
http://sunsite.unc.edu/elvis/elvishom.html
Graceland is one of America's favorite attractions. Go for a virtual visit.

261
Vacation Spot

http://www.wwte.com
http://www.vacationspot.com
These two sites will let you search for many types of vacations. You might find one that hits the spot.

262
Vacation Mall

http://www.onlinevacationmall.com
At this mall you can plan, price and buy your dream vacation.

263
What's Your Interest?

http://www.spectrav.com
If Specialty Travel doesn't have it listed, then it doesn't exist. From aerobics to zoology, you'll find it here.

264
Golf Travel Online

http://www.gto.com
http://golf.com/travel
http://www.resortgolfcourses.com
Combine two of our favorite pastimes: golf and travel.

265
Historical Travels

http://www.historytravel.com
Put some history in your next trip.

266
Historic Places

http://www.nr.nps.gov
The National Register Information System maintains the official database of historic places.

267
Camping Reservations

http://www.reserveusa.com

This is North America's largest camping reservation service. It offers over 49,500 camping facilities at 1,700 different locations managed by the USDA Forest Service and the U.S. Army Corps of Engineers.

268
Eco-Minded

http://www.ecosourcenetwork.com
http://www.ecotourism.org
http://www.ecotour.org

For the conservationist, ecotourism is your thing.

269
Great Adventures

http://www.specialtytravel.com

Here's a directory of adventure vacations and special interest travel worldwide. You'll find detailed information on thousands of unusual vacations.

270
Mountainous Terrain
http://www.mtsobek.com
Have a need for an adventurous mountain trip? Visit this site for some great ones.

271
Virtual Thrills
http://www.terraquest.com
You may never go there in the real world, so make a virtual visit to the Galapagos, Antarctica and other magnificent locations on our planet.

272
Wild Life Travel
http://www.worldwildlife.org/travel
Go to some of the best places on earth to see wildlife in its natural habitat.

273
Horse Sense

http://www.ridingtours.com
Do you love horses? Then you might want to take a horseback riding holiday.
This site offers tours all over the world.

274
Motorcycle Travelogue

http://www.trueamerica.com
Here's a travelogue written by Mark on his 19-month tour of the United
States. Vroom on over.

275
Great Outdoors

http://www.gorp.com
http://www.out-doors.com
Ah, the great outdoors. If it's outside, it's at these sites.

276
The Great Outdoors

http://www.greatoutdoors.com
If outdoor adventure is your thing, here is a leader in providing that
information to you.

277
National Scenic Byways

http://www.byways.org
The U.S. has some magnificent scenic roads. Can't get there today?
Then enjoy the slide show at this site.

278
Desert Storm

http://www.desertusa.com
Traveling to the desert? Here's a spot that will aid you.

279
Utah and Colorado

http://www.utah.com
http://www.skiutah.com
http://www.skicolorado.org
These two states are well-known for skiing, but they both offer much more.

280
Winter.com

http://www.iski.com
http://www.snowreport.com
http://www.skiconditions.com
http://www.iion.com/WinterNet/index.html
Your travel guides to the world of skiing. Check out the snow conditions and over 600 resorts.

281
Something's Fishy

http://www.fishsearch.com
If it ain't about fishing, it ain't here.

282
You'll Never Go There

http://www.envirolink.org/oneworld
These are locations you will probably never get to visit in the real world. So, check them out in the virtual world.

283
Smithsonian Travel

http://www.si.edu/tsa/sst
The Smithsonian offers the largest, most diverse museum-based educational travel program in the United States and carefully designs 360 tours to 250 destinations worldwide each year.

284
Gear Up

http://www.rei.com
http://www.rei-outlet.com
http://www.rei.com/OUT_THERE/OUTLINKS/outlink.html
Wear the right stuff.

CHAPTER VIII
TRAVEL MEDIA AND RESOURCES

285
Relax with Travel and Leisure

http://www.pathfinder.com/travel

Time Warner has one of the most in-depth sites on the Net. Its travel edition is guaranteed to be a great companion.

286
Leisure Travel News

http://www.ttgweb.com

Here's a newspaper for the leisure travel industry that contains timely and interesting articles for all types of travel and geographic areas.

287
Newspapers Everywhere

http://www.thepaperboy.com
http://newo.com/news
http://www.newslink.org
http://www.all-links.com/newscentral

There are many great newspapers on the Net. You can find them here.

288
Travel with the Times

http://www.nytoday.com
http://www.nytimes.com/travel
http://www.nytimes.com/library/travel/whatsdoing/index.html

One of the finest newspapers in the world would love to assist you with your travel news and information.

289
USA Today Travel
http://www.usatoday.com/life/travel/ltfront.htm
From articles to tips about travel, USA Today has it for you.

290
The Travel Channel
http://www.travelchannel.com
A great resource on TV, this Net version is also very useful.

291
Travel Update
http://www.travelupdate.com
Travel with this TV show. Make sure you click on the Travel Guide section.

292
Savvy Talk

http://www.savvytraveler.org
Rudy Maxa is the host of The Savvy Traveler talk show. Listen and learn about great travel spots throughout the world.

293
Radio Journal

http://www.travelersjournal.com
The Traveler's Journal is a series of two-minute audio programs broadcast daily via public radio. Using RealAudio, you can listen to short but informative travel information.

294
It's a Holiday

http://www.travelholiday.com
If you want travel tips, articles and exciting trips to take, make sure you go to this site.

295
Be An Insider
http://www.insiders.com
Insider has the inside scoop on many cities. Check it out to see if it has a city that interests you.

296
How to See the World
http://www.artoftravel.com
This is a complete online book about backpacking around the world.

297
High Brow Travel
http://www.salon.com/travel
Salon Magazine is happy to provide excellent travel reporting for the discriminating traveler.

298
Travel Rag

http://www.travelmag.co.uk
Check out stories by professional traveloguers as well as commoners.

299
Travel the Net

http://www.travelthe.net
Every week, get to read an article about traveling somewhere in the world.

300
Magazines Galore

http://www.kasbah.com/traveltoolbox/travelmagazines.htm
http://www.zinezone.com/zones/travel
Lots of travel magazines are on the Net. Check out these listings, and read to your heart's content.

INDEX (BY SITE NUMBER)